LANDSCAPES
PAINTING BY NUMBERS

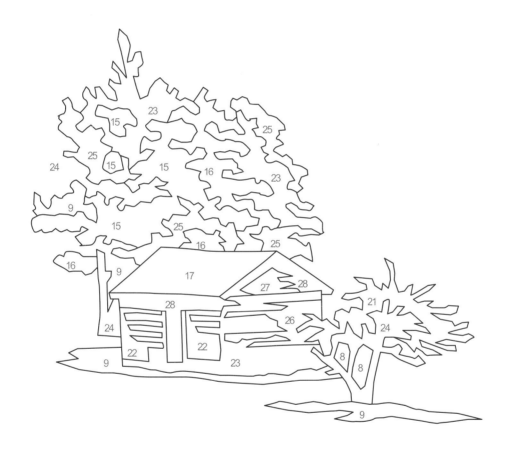

David Woodroffe

SIRIUS

SIRIUS

This edition published in 2021 by Sirius Publishing, a division of
Arcturus Publishing Limited,
26/27 Bickels Yard, 151–153 Bermondsey Street,
London SE1 3HA

ISBN: 978-1-3988-0772-3
CH007286NT
Supplier 29, Date 0521, Print run 11231

Printed in China

Created for children 10+

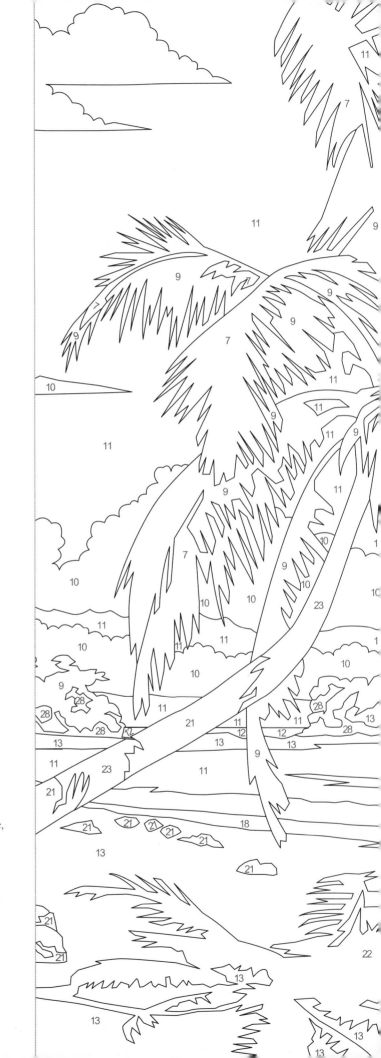

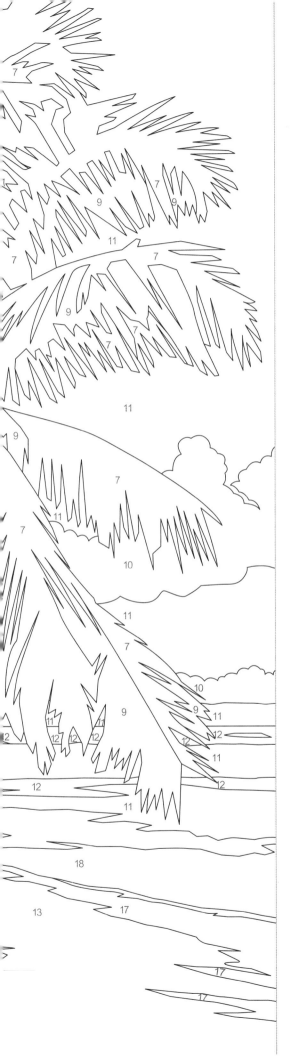

Introduction

Whether a Japanese bridge in a manicured garden or a lighthouse atop a rocky outcrop or migratory geese flying through a Nordic forest, there are a host of landscapes for you to explore in this painting-by-numbers book. Comforting scenes such as a flower meadow, or a church seen across an open field, contrast with a walker on a precipitous mountain road, and palm trees swaying in a tropical landscape. All should provide inspiration for you to explore your painting technique and hone it to create a beautiful finished artwork.

Painting by numbers is a great way to begin to exercise your artistic talents and gain confidence in using paint, as well as an understanding of how an artwork is constructed. The illustrations here are printed on heavyweight art paper suitable for a range of different kinds of paints.

Each image is fully numbered so that you can build up an impressive artwork. Using the key on the inside cover, match your paints to the shades in the key. If there is no number that means the space should be left white or filled with white paint. Painting these images, especially the more complex scenes, will take time and patience, but it will be very rewarding to see your pictures take shape.

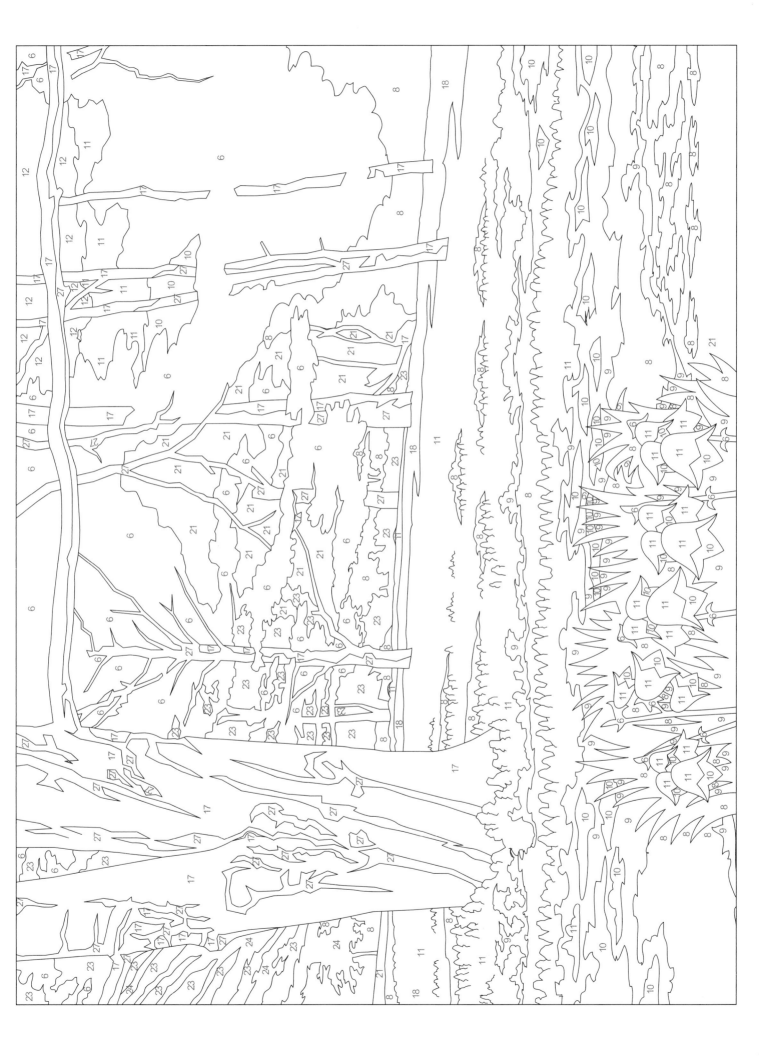

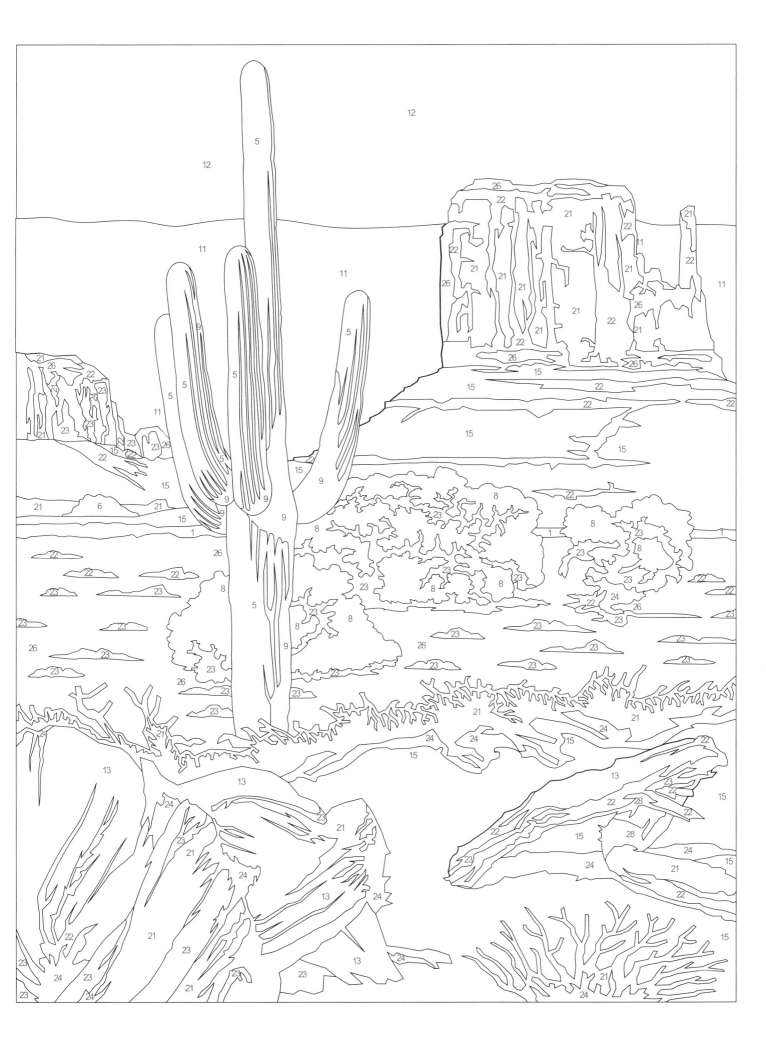

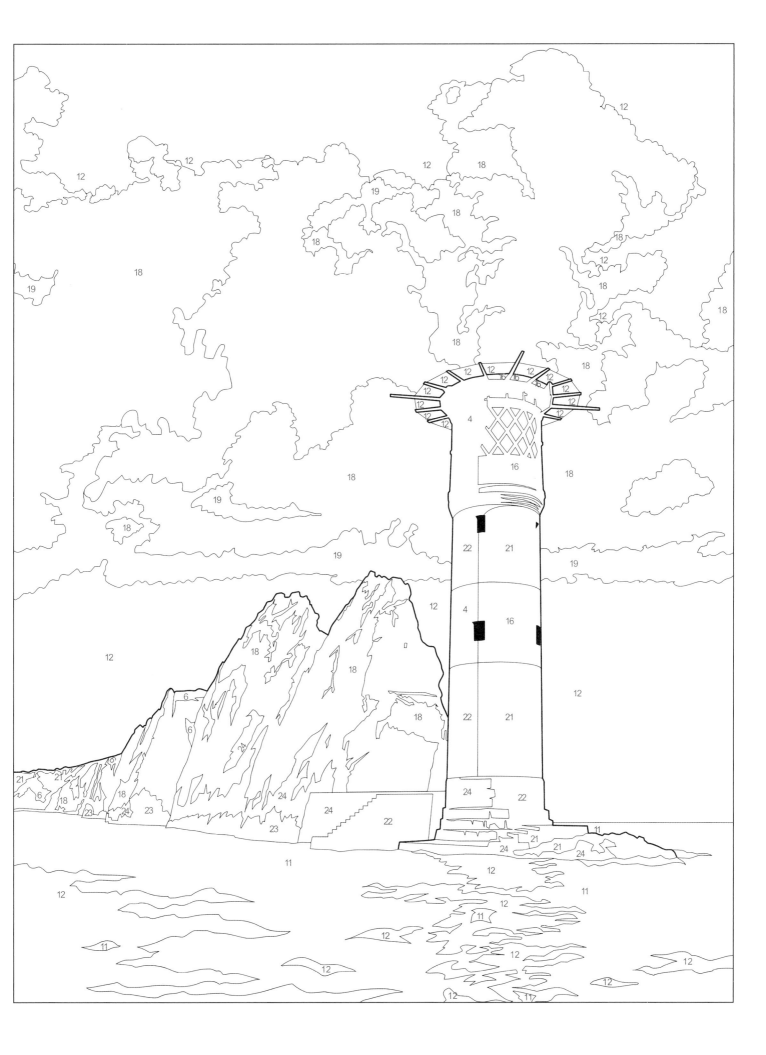

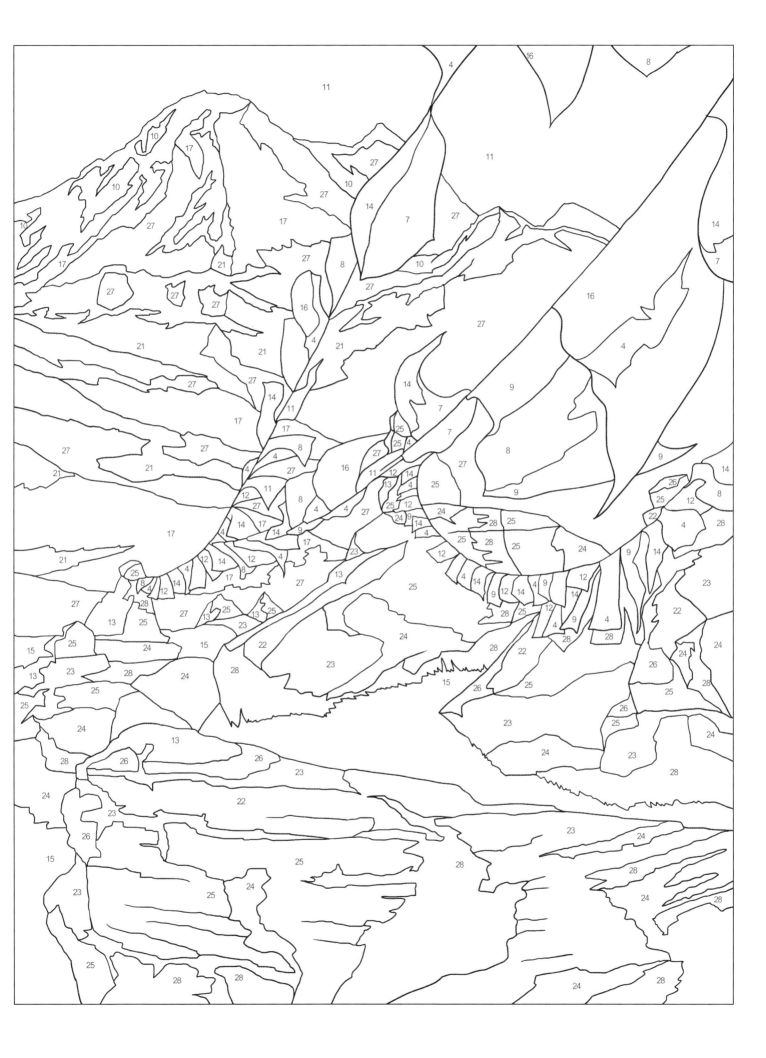

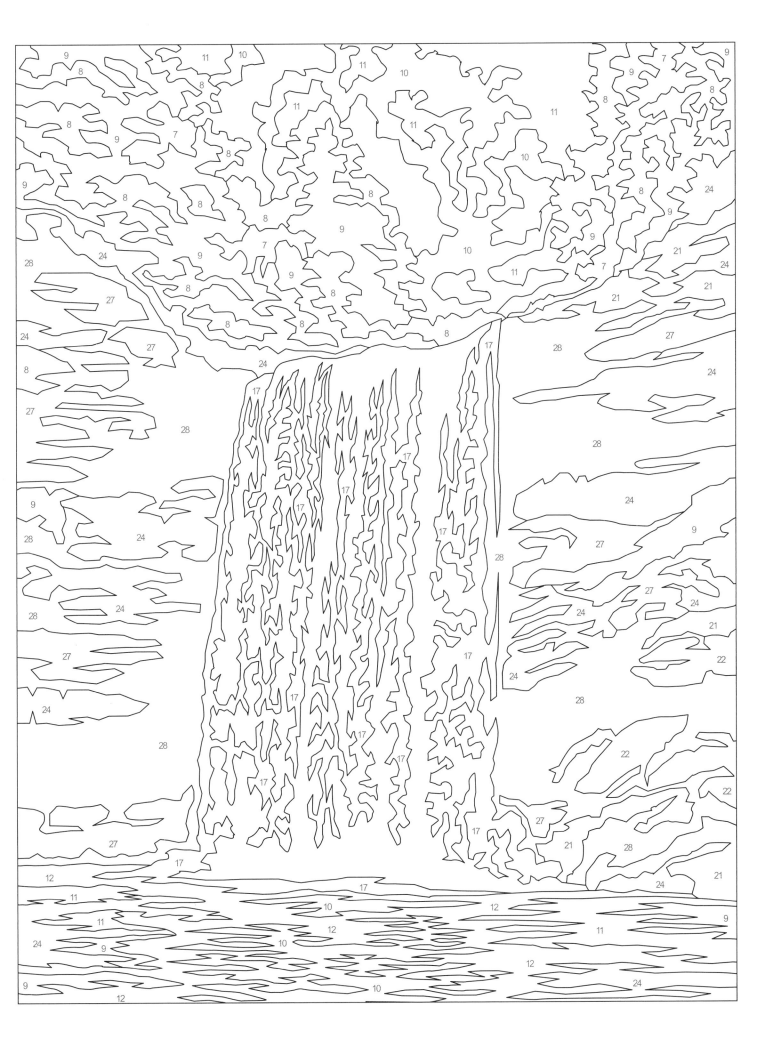

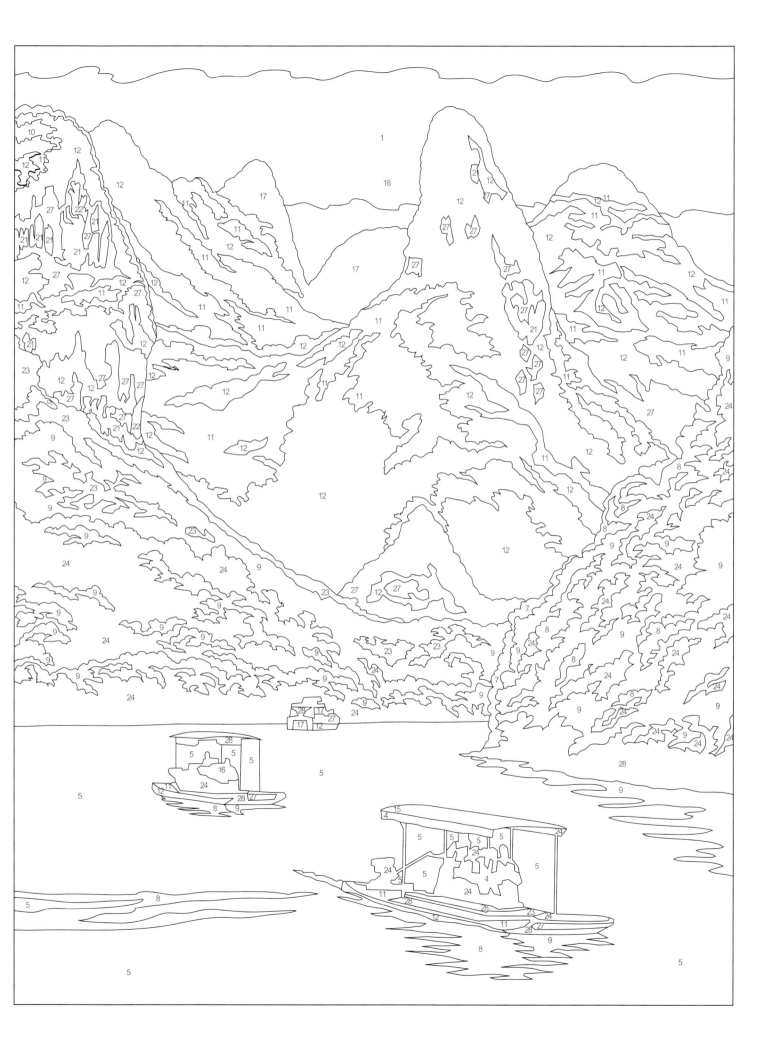

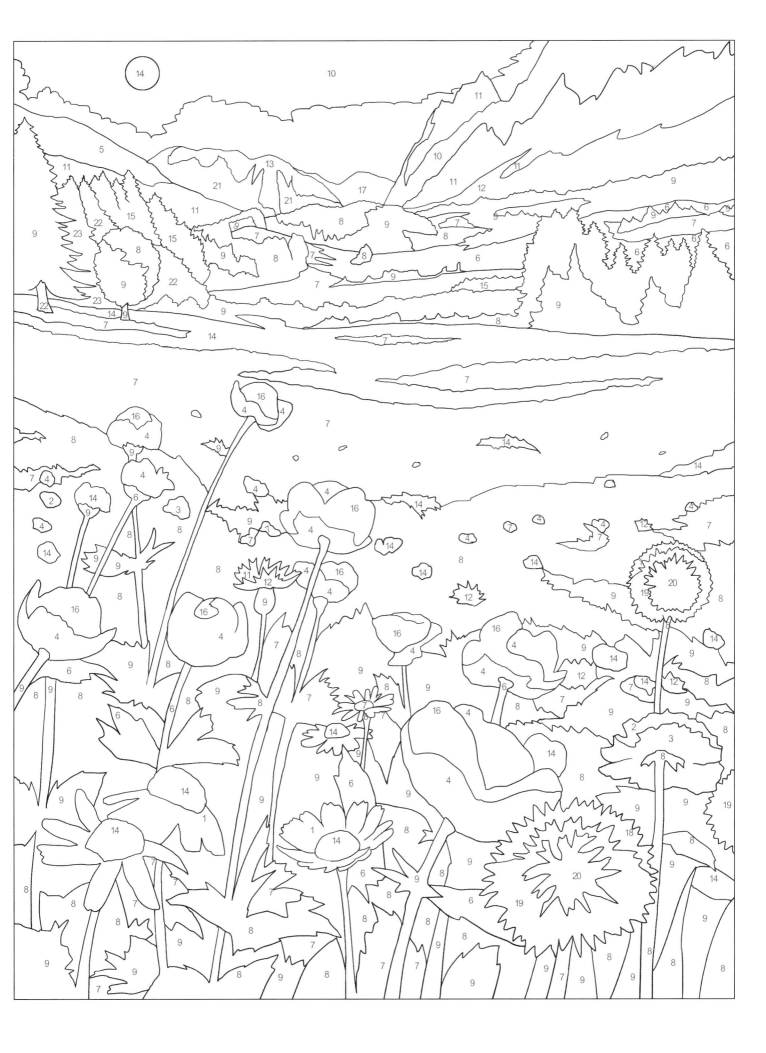

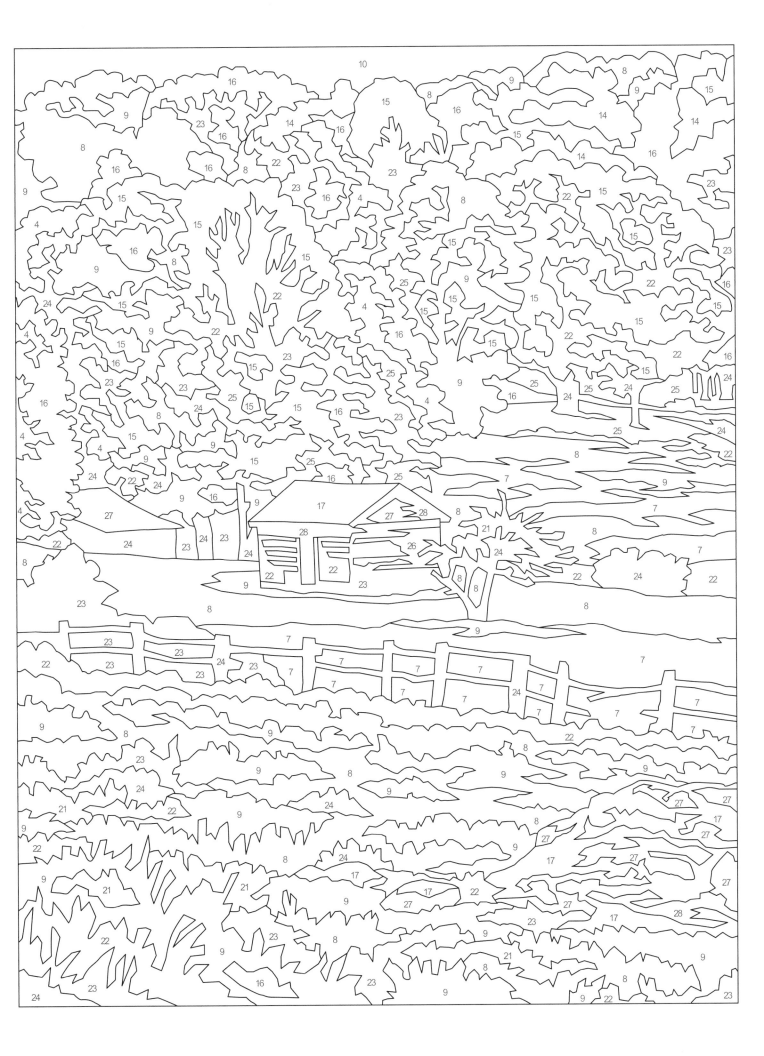

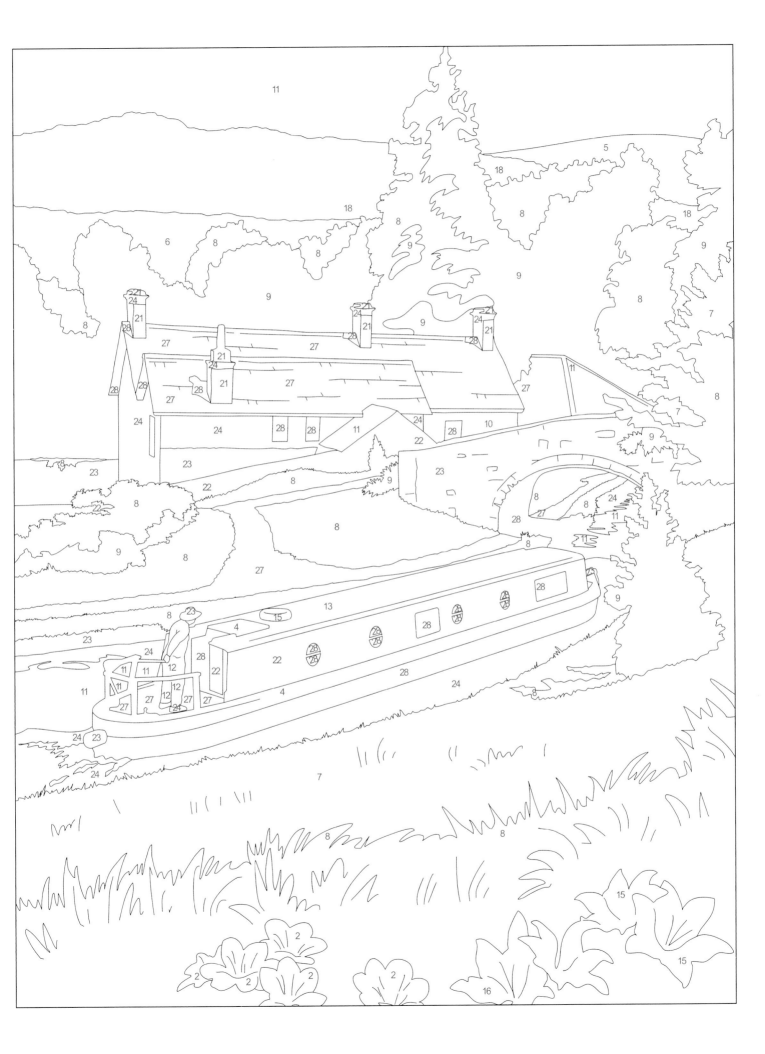

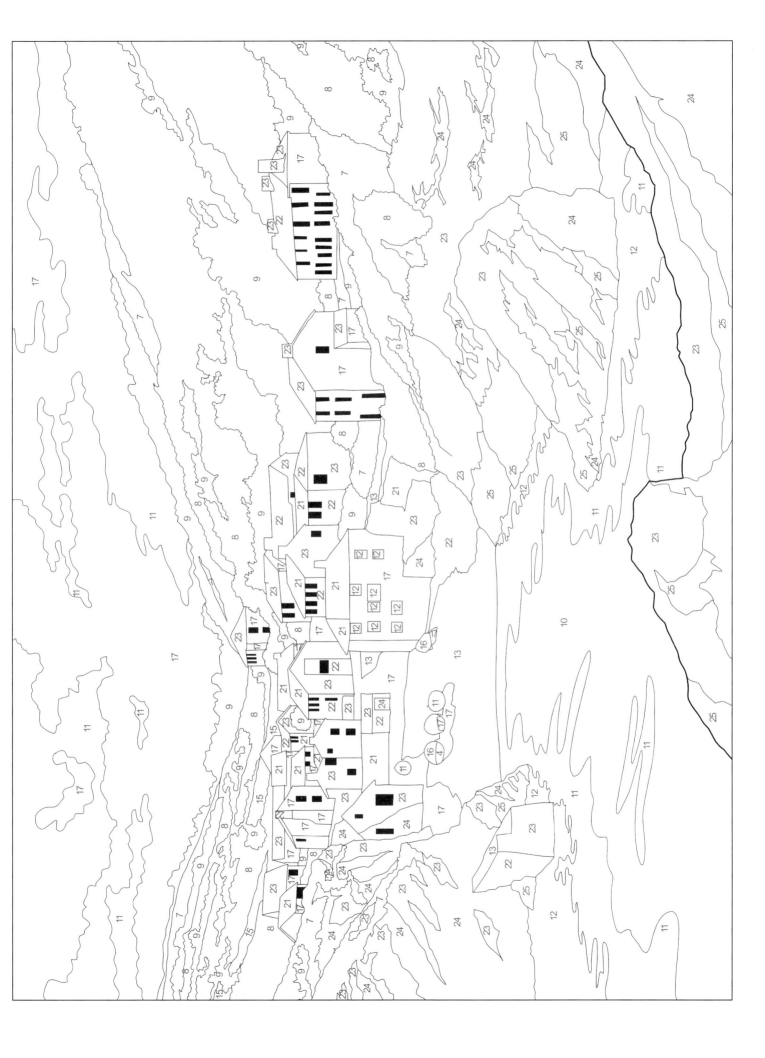

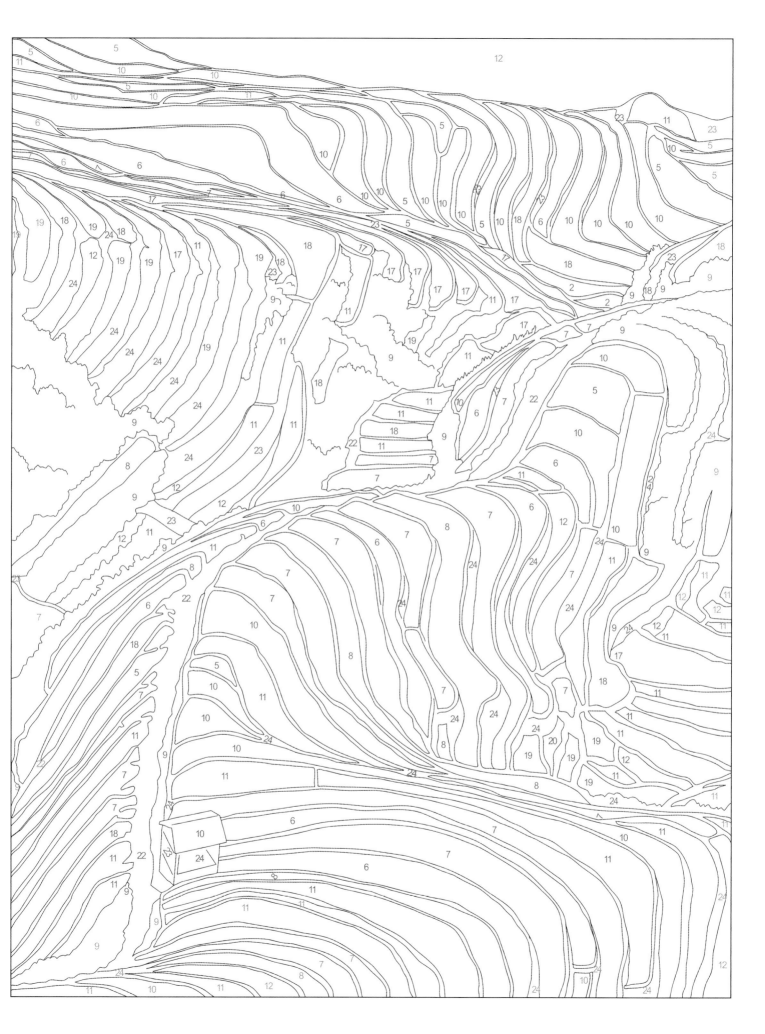

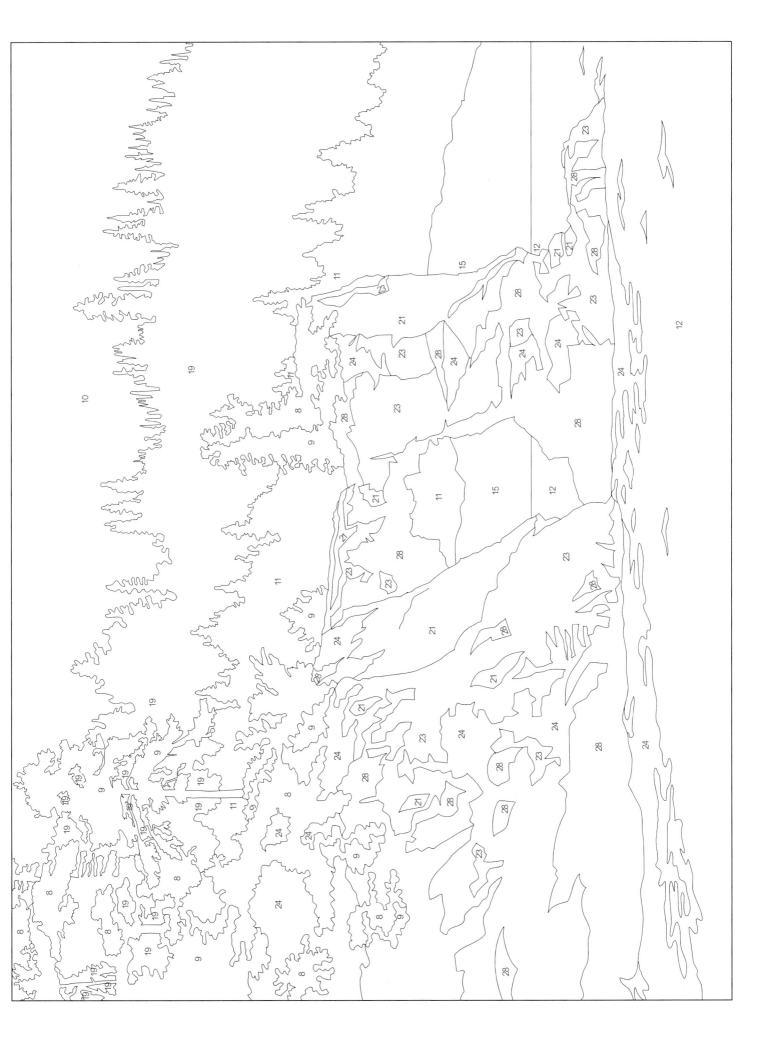

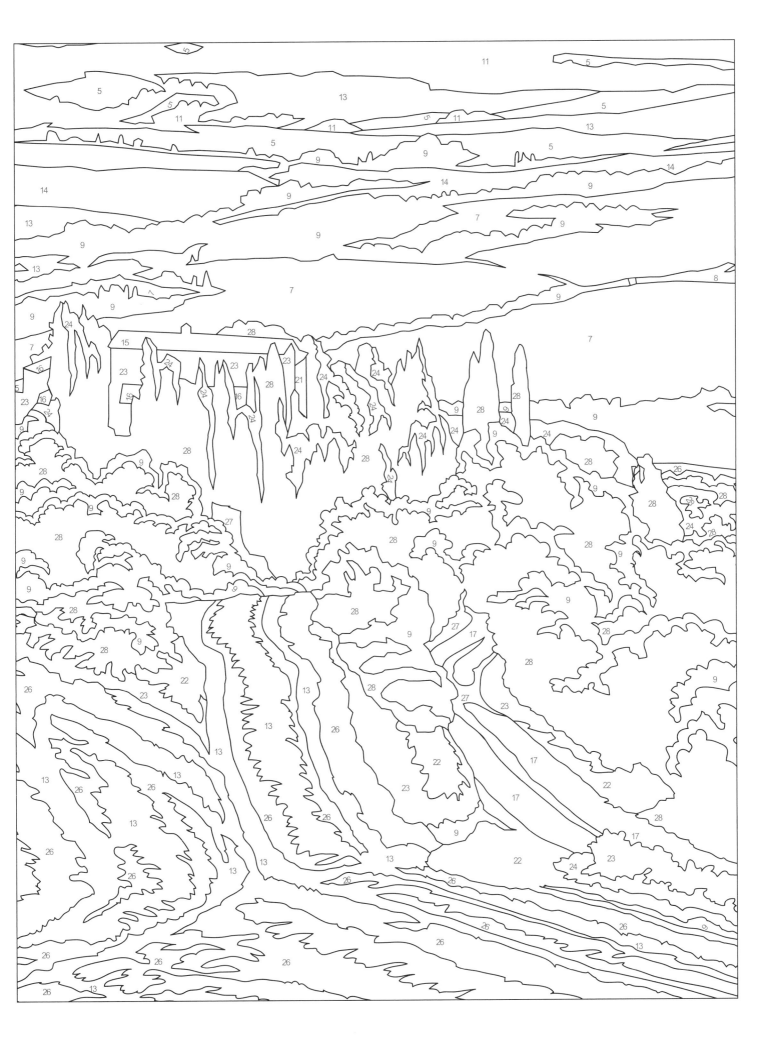

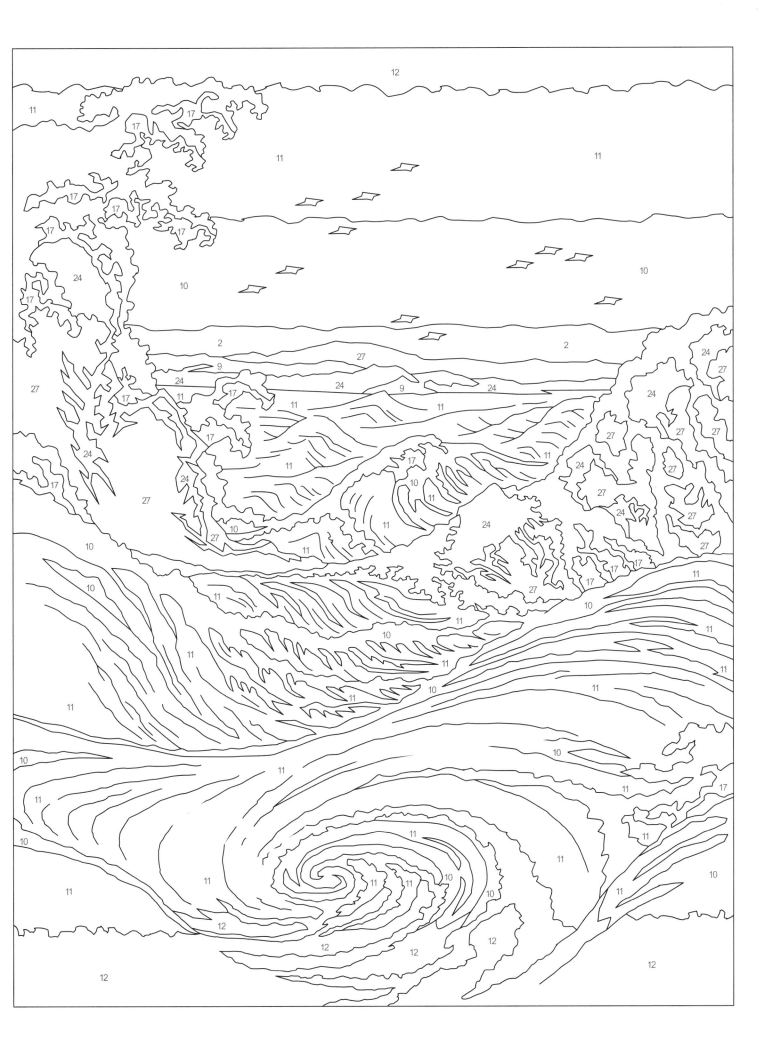

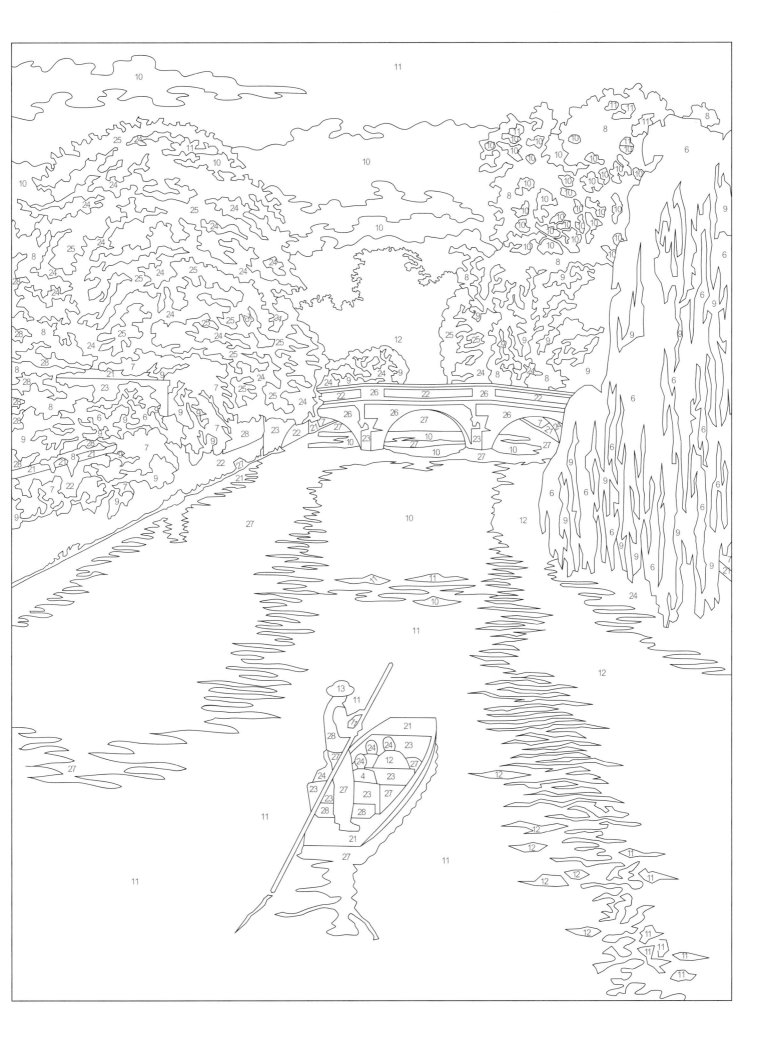

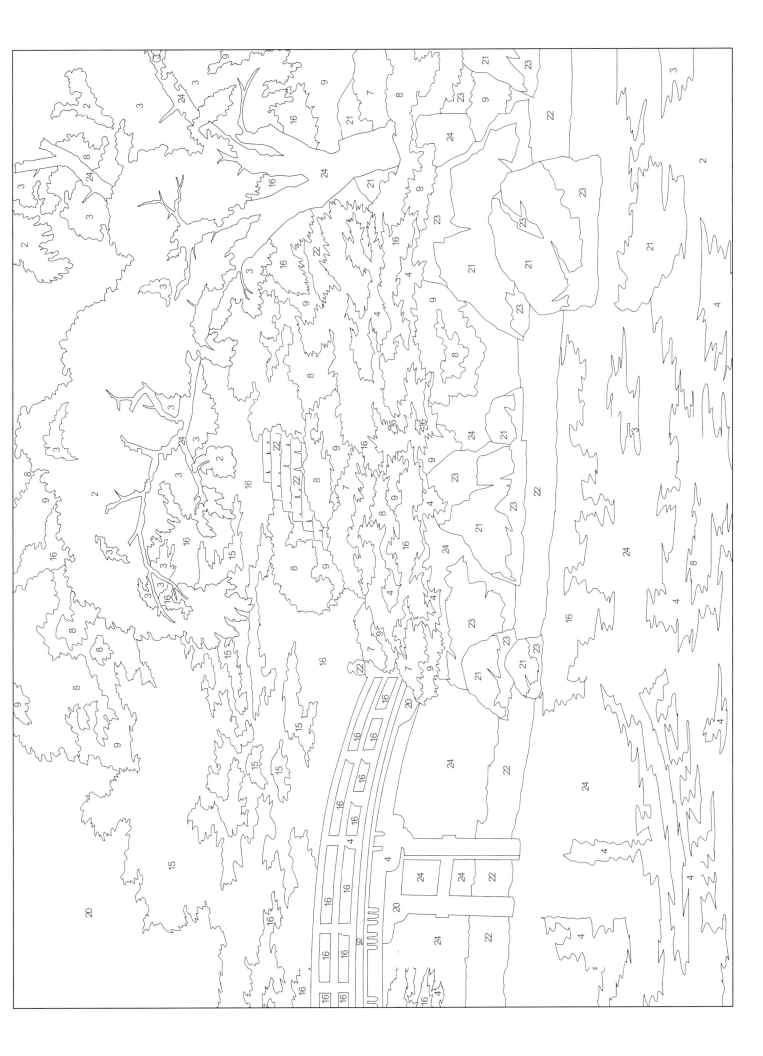

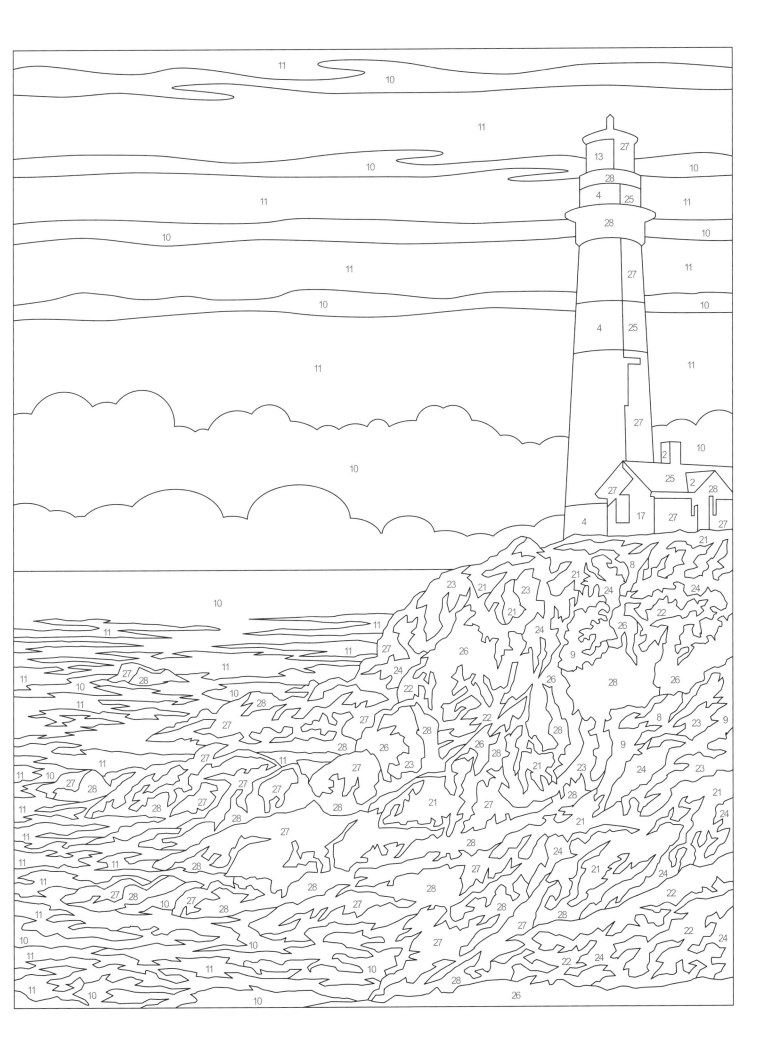

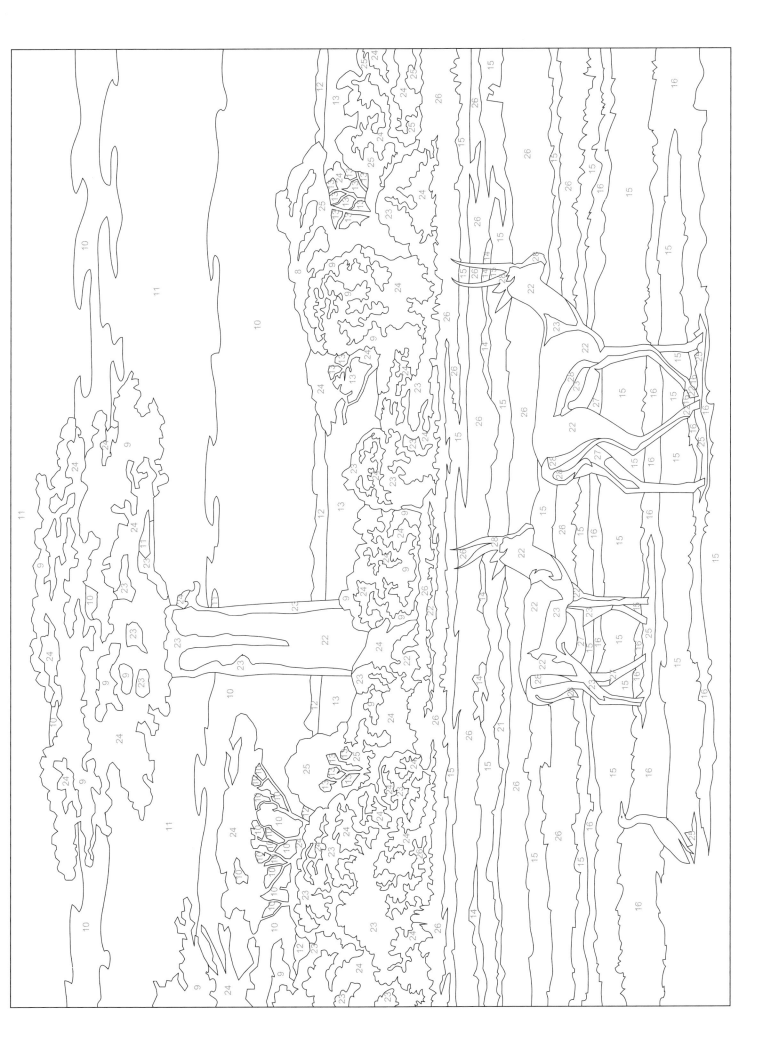

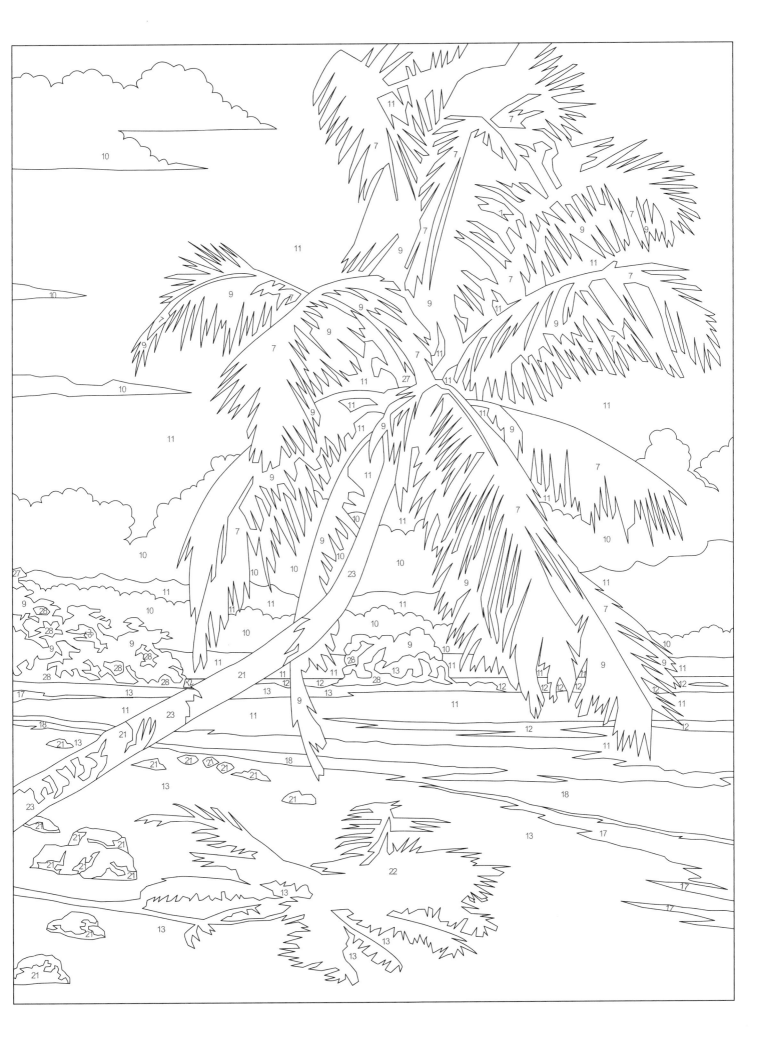

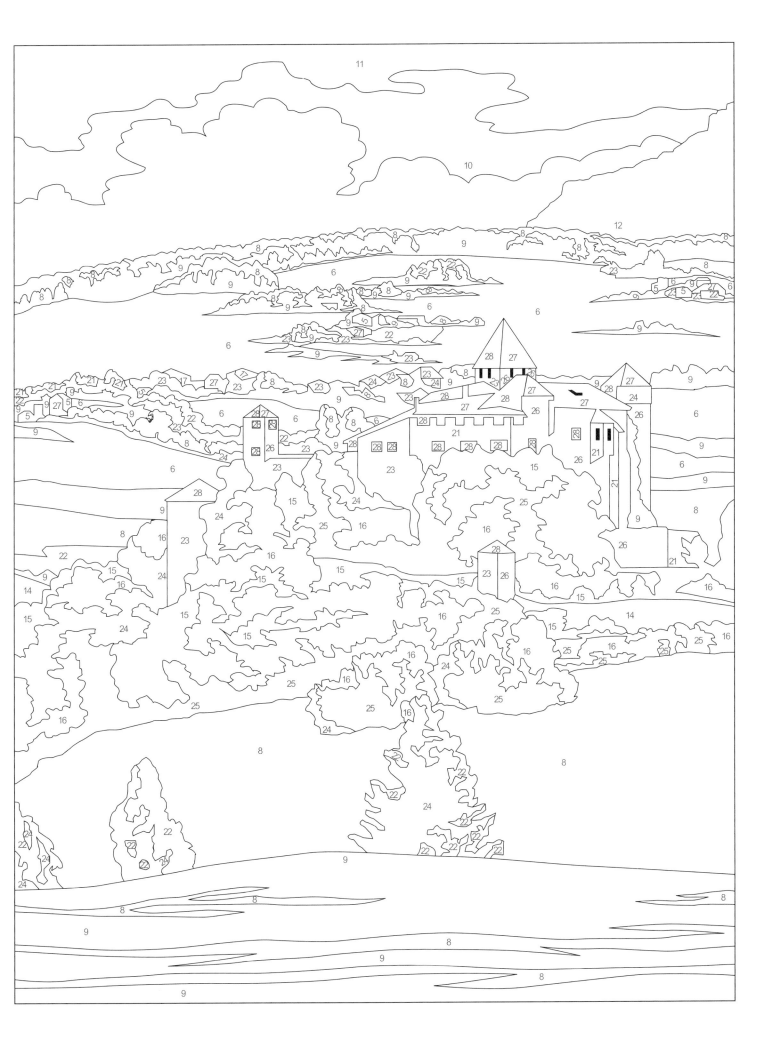

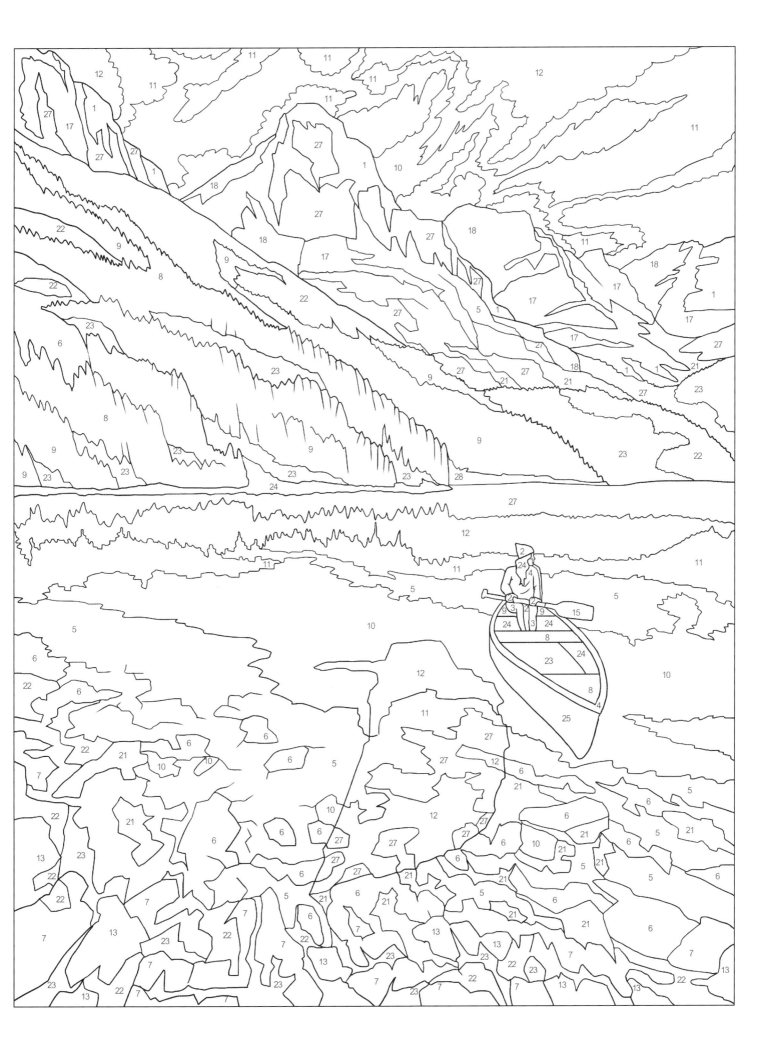

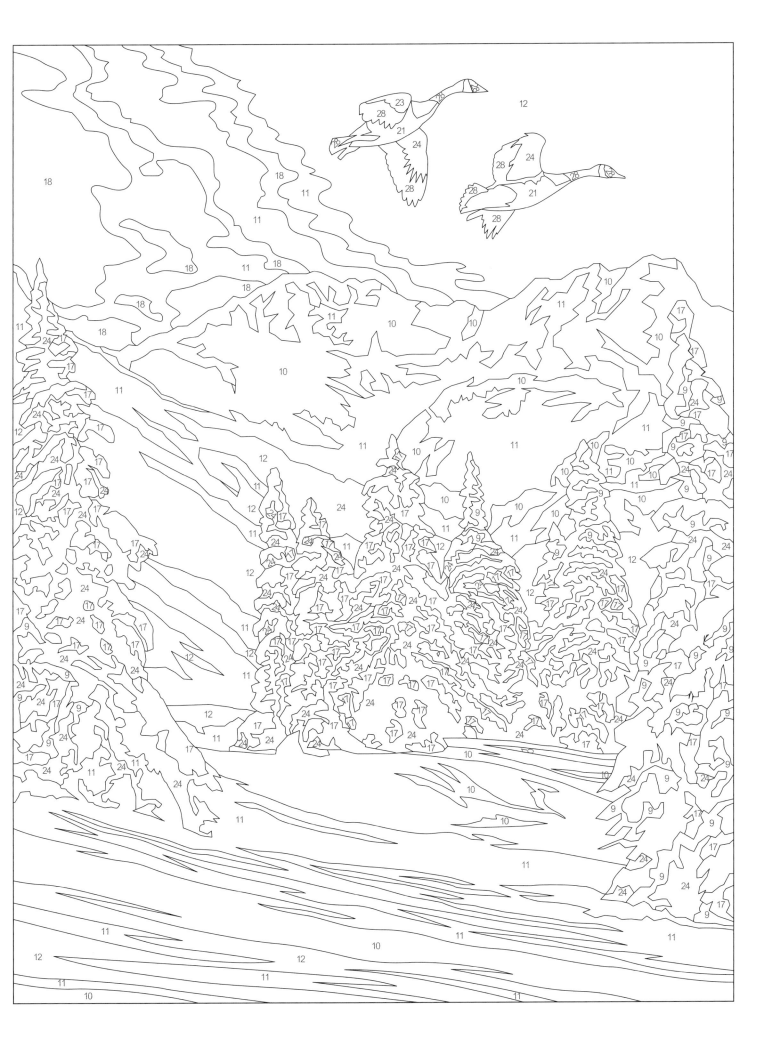

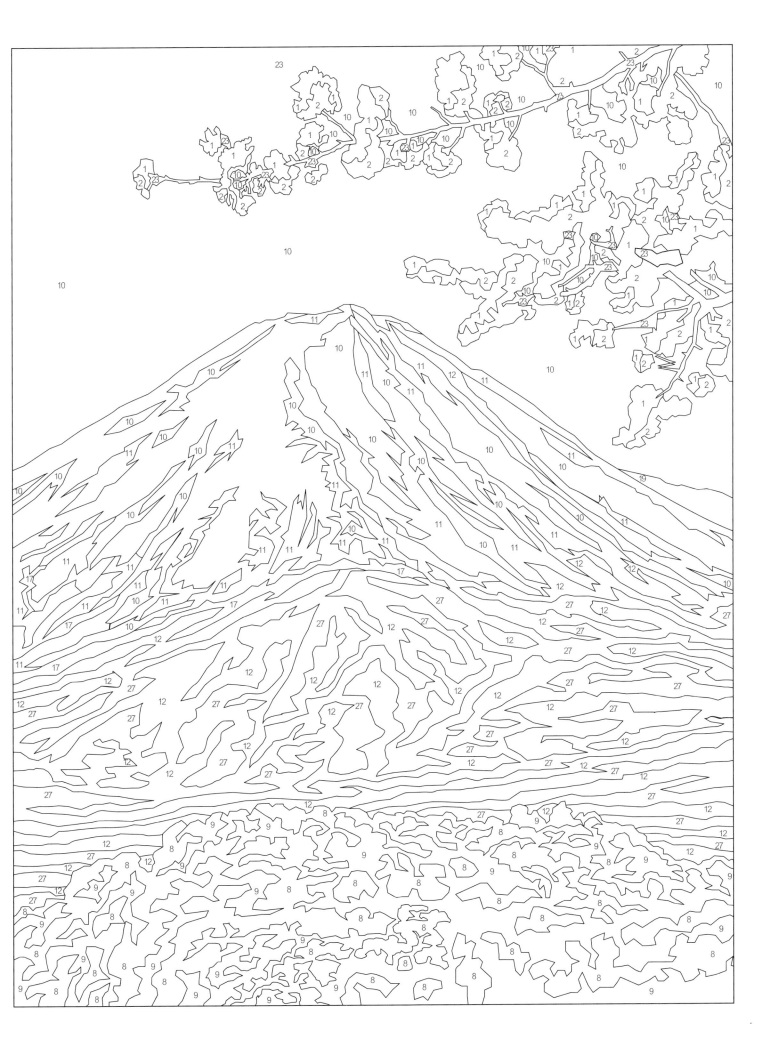

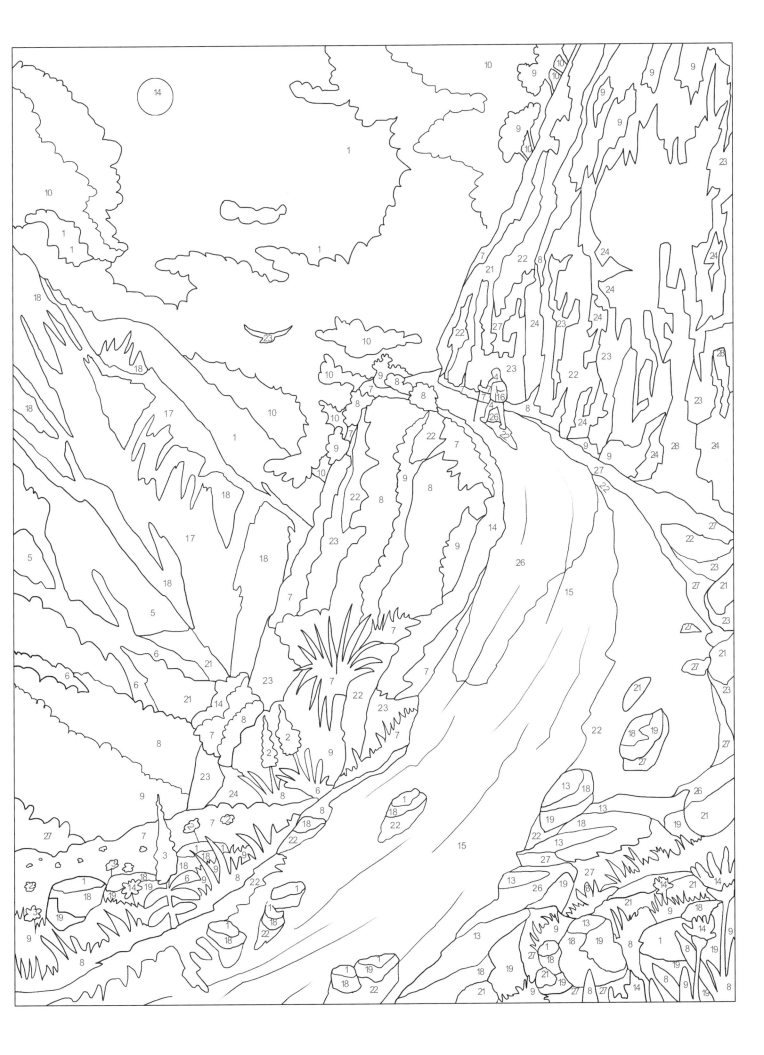

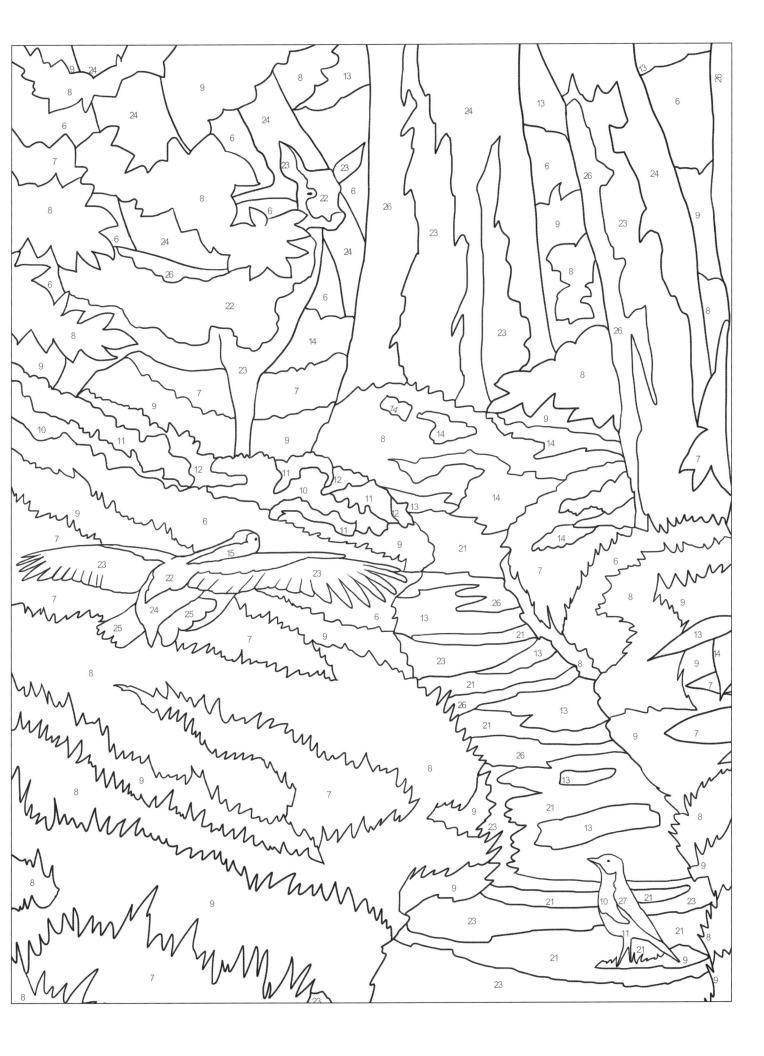

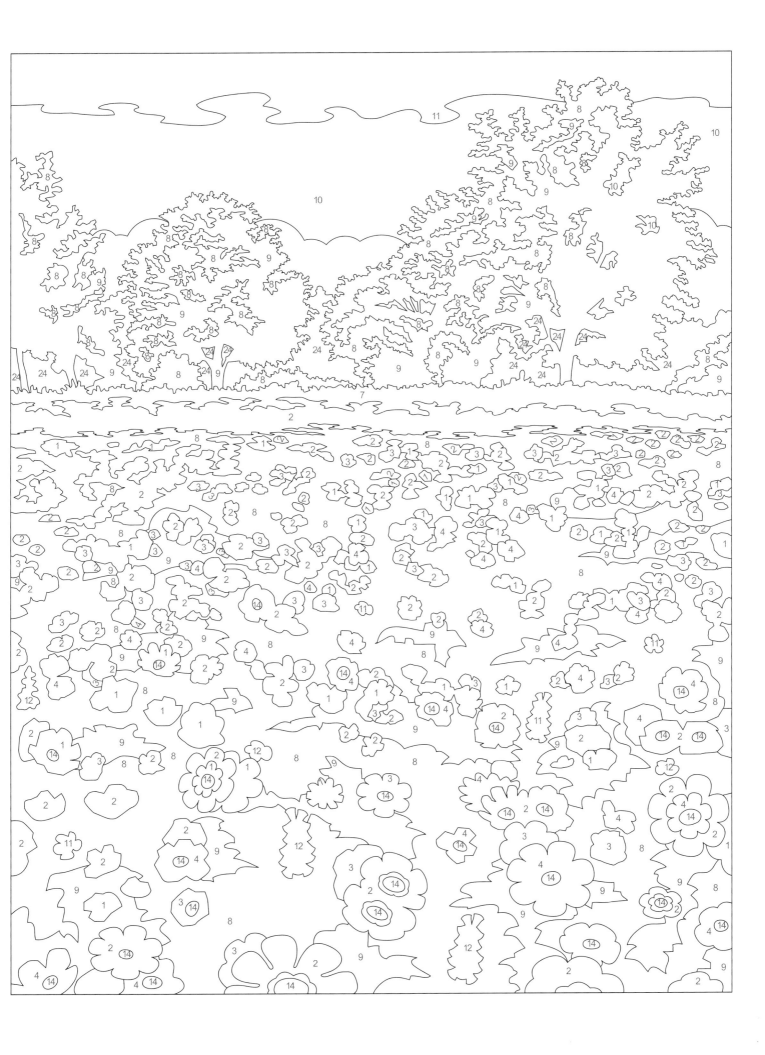

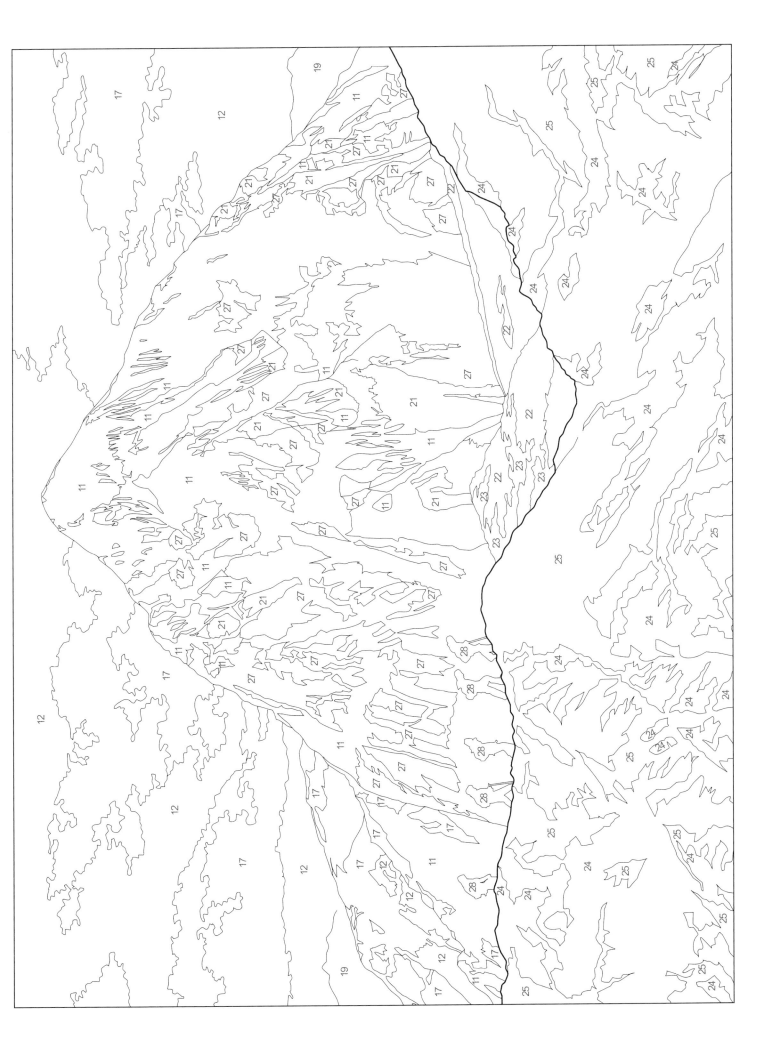

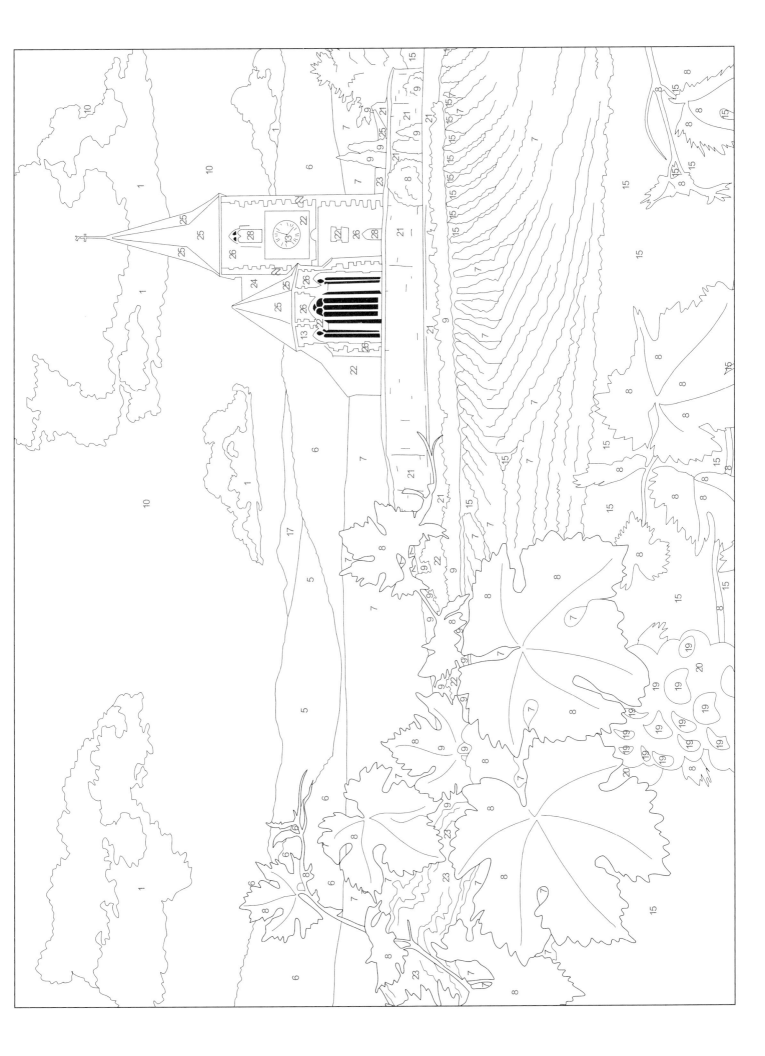

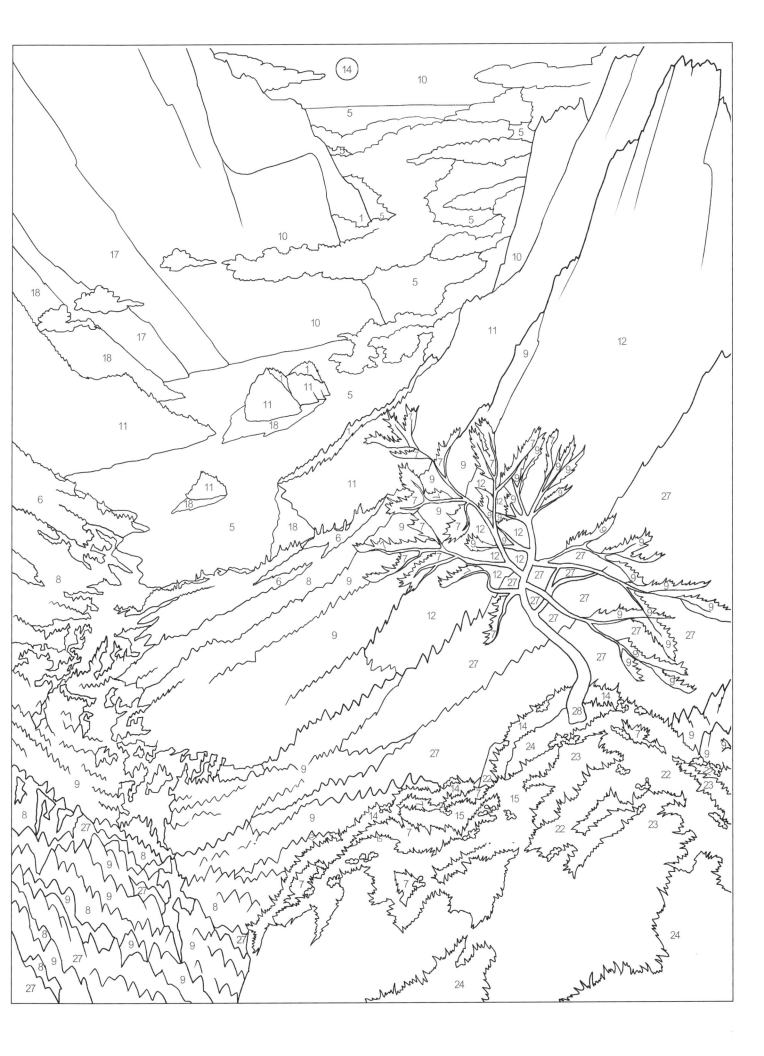